DISCARD

W9-CKL-187

GIFT 8-7-13

–Shoals on the Catawba River at Landsford Canal State Park

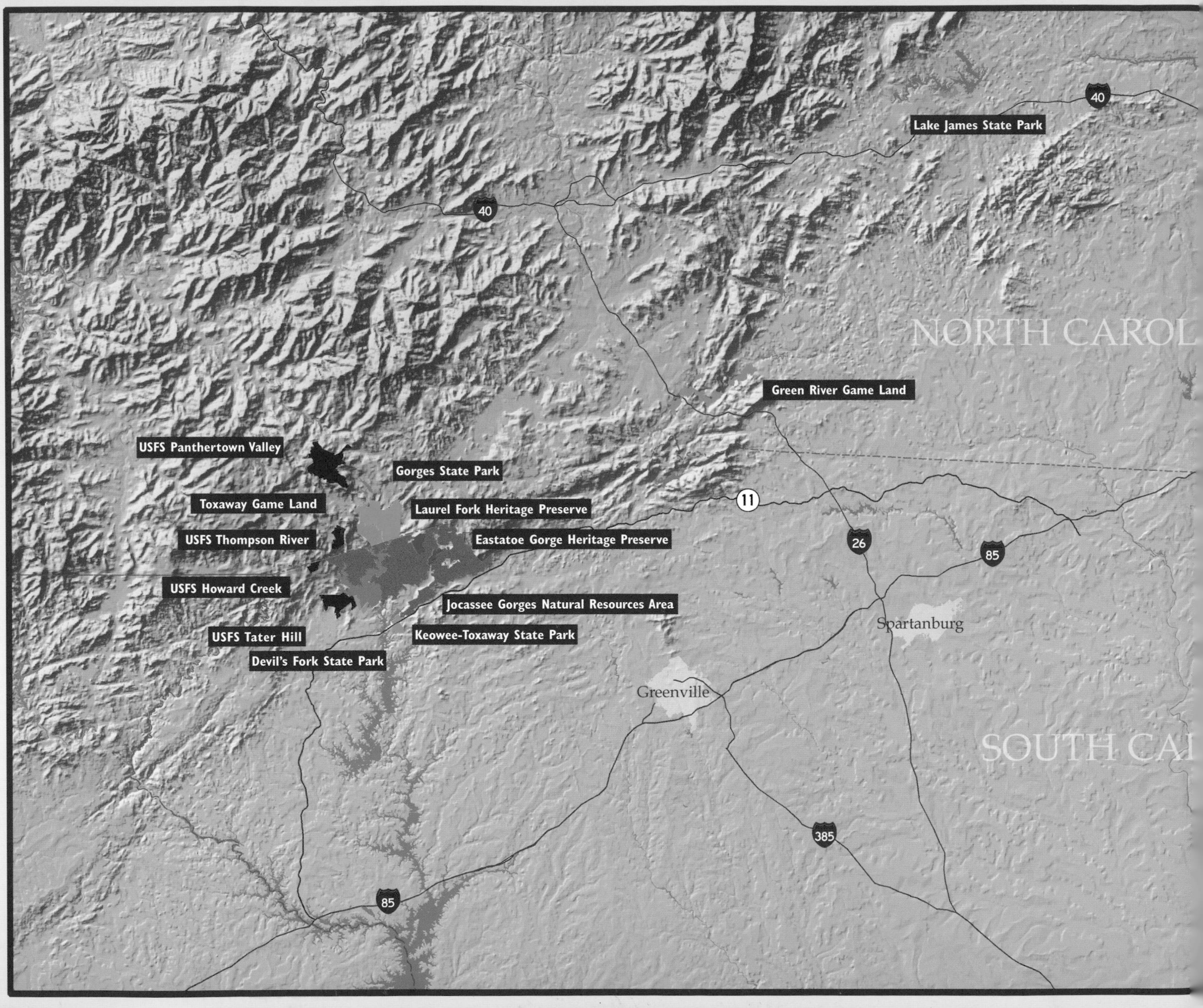

Lake James State Park

NORTH CAROL

Green River Game Land

USFS Panthertown Valley

Gorges State Park

Toxaway Game Land

Laurel Fork Heritage Preserve

USFS Thompson River

Eastatoe Gorge Heritage Preserve

11

26

85

USFS Howard Creek

Jocassee Gorges Natural Resources Area

Spartanburg

USFS Tater Hill

Keowee-Toxaway State Park

Devil's Fork State Park

Greenville

SOUTH CAI

385

85

40

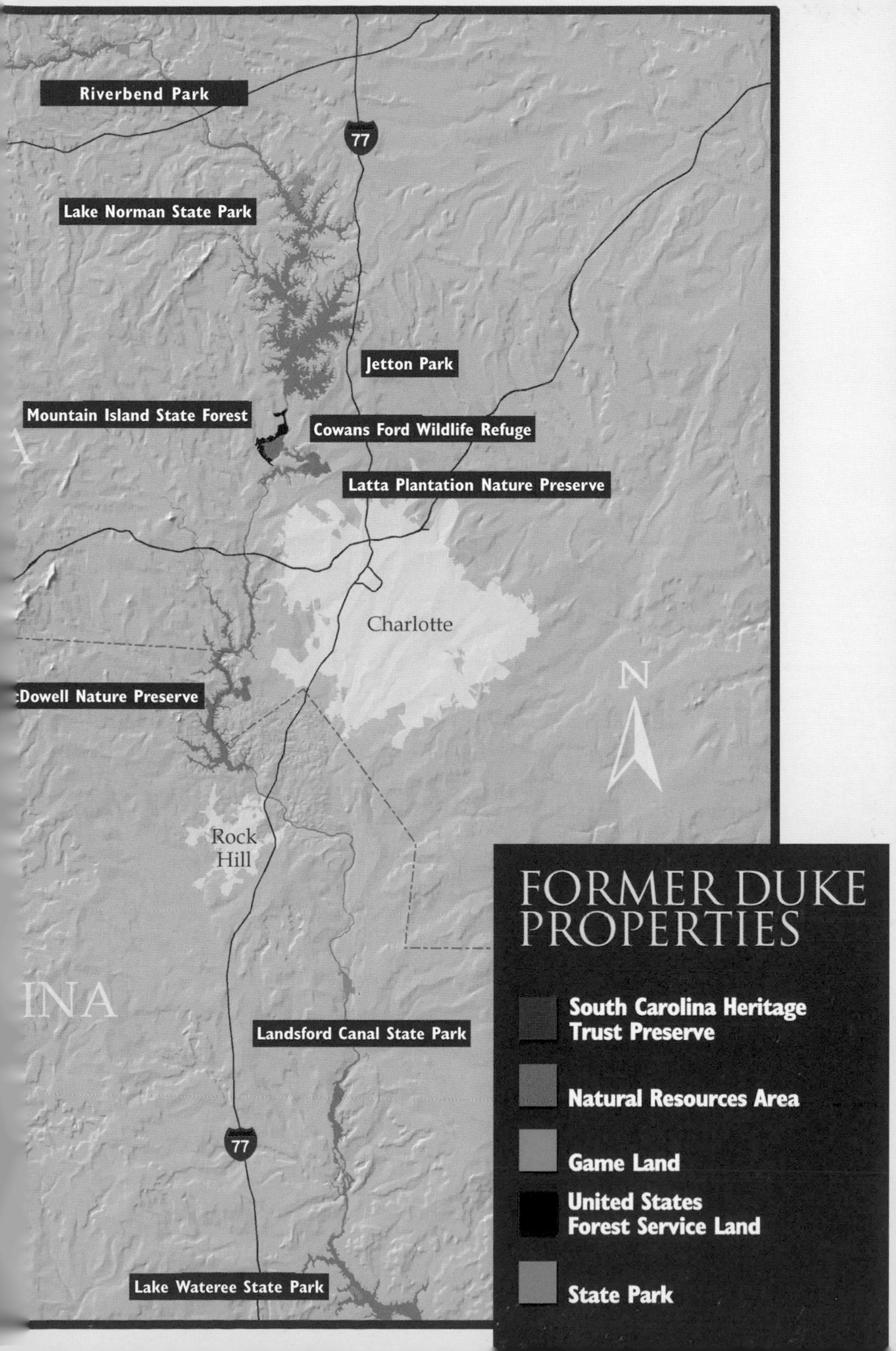

Riverbend Park

Lake Norman State Park

Jetton Park

Mountain Island State Forest

Cowans Ford Wildlife Refuge

Latta Plantation Nature Preserve

Charlotte

cDowell Nature Preserve

Rock
Hill

INA

Landsford Canal State Park

Lake Wateree State Park

N

FORMER DUKE PROPERTIES

South Carolina Heritage
Trust Preserve

Natural Resources Area

Game Land

United States
Forest Service Land

State Park

MOSAIC

Cabarrus County Public Library
www.cabarruscounty.us/library

MOSAIC

21 Special Places in the Carolinas

The Land Conservation Legacy of Duke Power

PHOTOGRAPHY AND TEXT BY

THOMAS WYCHE

WESTCLIFFE PUBLISHERS

www.westcliffepublishers.com

Text and Photography: © 2002 C. Thomas Wyche. All rights reserved.

Editor: Sallie Greenwood
Designer: Paulette Livers, Livers Lambert Design

Published by:
Westcliffe Publishers, Inc.
P.O. Box 1261
Englewood, CO 80150
www.westcliffepublishers.com

Printed in Hong Kong through World Print, Ltd.

No portion of this book, either text or photography, may be reproduced in any form,
including electronically, without the express written permission of the publisher.

International Standard Book Number: 1-56579-426-5

For more information about other fine books and calendars from Westcliffe Publishers,
please contact your local bookstore, call us at 1-800-523-3692, write for our
free color catalog, or visit us on the Web at www.westcliffepublishers.com.

Contents

Left, Tranquility in the Blue Ridge Mountains from Lake James State Park
Right, Auger Fork Creek Waterfall, Gorges State Park
Preceding page, View of Mountain Island Lake

Foreword

For nearly a century, Duke Power has been a proud partner in the steward-ship of the Carolinas' natural resources. Through the years, we have worked with others who share our commitment to the environment and to our communities to ensure that future generations will be able to enjoy and appreciate the rare beauty of this land we call home.

Duke Power has contributed to public conservation the ownership of approximately 40,000 acres in South Carolina and 29,000 acres in North Carolina. We've helped preserve lands along the Savannah, Green, Tuckaseegee, and Catawba Rivers or their tributaries.

Within these pages, Thomas Wyche's stunning photographs capture the lands that are part of this generation's legacy, from stirring forests of the Jocassee Gorges to the crystal waters of Lake James State Park. We also find interesting cultural, historical, and botanical facts about each area, as well as directions that tell us how to find them.

Numerous public agencies, land trusts, conservancy groups, and local governments joined forces to protect these and other natural resources and to preserve lands and open spaces for all of us to enjoy. We are pleased to be a part in this effort. We well know that being a responsible corporate citizen means finding ways to balance environmental protection with economic vitality. Both are essential to our quality of life. Both are part of the living legacy we leave behind.

—Bill Coley, President
Duke Power
July 29, 2001

Opposite, Sweet Shrub—a fragrant plant of mountain coves
Right, Butterfly Pea—a showy flower of piedmont pine forests

Introduction

The word "conservation" brings different things to mind. However, one topic that most people today would agree is very pertinent to any discussion on conservation is the protection of undeveloped land—open green space that might include important natural or historical resources. Local, state, and federal resource agencies are routinely involved in efforts to acquire important lands for conservation. The intense interest of these agencies and the relatively recent creation of numerous private land trusts are indications of the interest and needs associated with providing public conservation lands.

At Duke Power, for the nearly 100 years of our existence, we have been directly involved with the acquisition and management of land for the core business activity of generating electricity for our service area in the piedmont and foothills regions of the two Carolinas. In doing this work we have acquired lands for reservoirs, power plants sites, and related facilities. Our use of these utility lands is regulated through appropriate statutes associated with Duke Power's role as an electric utility company.

By the 1970s, Duke had also acquired more than 250,000 acres of lands that were not part of our electric generation plans but separate company assets. Duke has managed these lands over the decades and has made various uses of them. Today, in the year 2001, as our company approaches its 100th anniversary, we are pleased to report that approximately 69,000 acres of these non-utility lands have been placed into permanent conservation protection and are now under the ownership and management of

county, state, and federal resource agencies. These previously owned Company holdings have become some of our region's highest quality state parks, state forests, state wildlife management areas, U.S. Forest Service lands, and county parks. They contain some of our region's unique natural/cultural/recreational resources and are being managed on a daily basis by agency resource experts to ensure their long-term protection. And, most importantly, these lands are available for the general public to visit, to enjoy, to hunt, fish, and hike on, and to learn from. They are places of beauty for a family picnic, to swim, wade a stream, and to learn about nature and/or cultural history. They are for people and our native wildlife.

We have accomplished these important conservation efforts through our internal business processes and through the effective partnerships and working relationships that we have with many personnel of the resource agencies and environmental groups of the Carolinas. Without the patience, hard work, and cooperative nature of these dedicated personnel, these successful results would not

have been possible. We are very proud of these effective conservation partnerships, of our Duke Power teams who have worked with them, and the resulting legacy of land conservation that together they have produced. That legacy is the subject of this book.

—*Buddy Davis, Vice-President*
Environment, Health and Safety
Duke Power
August 2001

Left, Witchhazel, a winter blossom
Opposite, Drawbar Cliffs, part of the Jocassee Gorges

Preface

OVERVIEW

Hugging the border of South Carolina and North Carolina and scattered along the Catawba River are twenty-one nature preserves, wildlife management areas, and parks, all formerly owned by Duke Power Company. Collectively, they are a wonder of natural wilderness areas. Some of them are on the Blue Ridge Escarpment, alongside rushing streams and waterfalls; some of them offer exciting challenges to hikers, campers, or hunters; others provide pockets of solitude for those who prefer a more tranquil outdoor experience. Still other preserves in the rolling hills of the piedmont border quiet streams and lakes of the Catawba River watershed.

Combined, these beautiful forested lands exceed 69,000 acres, permanently protected as a habitat for plants and animals and as places of recreation for anyone. *Diverse in size and location, these twenty-one natural areas form a mosaic of special places that is unique in beauty and history. The story of the formation of this unique mosaic—an aggregate of pristine wilderness and recreation areas—deserves to be told.*

BACKGROUND

Looking back over several generations, one wonders why it was not obvious that our earth's resources are limited. How could it escape our attention that unless trees were planted to replace those being cut, we would soon have no more lumber? Or that the air we breathe, our streams, and our oceans

Opposite, Silhouettes and sunset
Right, Dwarf Iris

would be poisoned by continuing to pour wastes into them? In looking back, however, it is clear that the obvious, if considered at all, was largely ignored by many.

The foothills and piedmont areas of the Carolinas were not immune to some of the negative effects of population growth and rapid industrialization. During the early twentieth century, the logging industry was well on its way to denuding the entire Appalachian Mountain forests from Pennsylvania to Georgia, and there were no plans for reforestation. Uncontrolled hunting had already extirpated herds of buffalo and elk from the Carolinas, and the Carolina parakeet and the passenger pigeon, whose flocks had once darkened the skies, were also erased from existence. Then current farming practices led to entire farms in the Midwest blowing away as the Dust Bowl darkened the landscape. Southern cotton farming and its destructive techniques allowed topsoil to be washed away, leaving huge, deep gullies impossible to cultivate. Pollutants were poisoning the air and the rivers. An extreme example of environmental irresponsibility occurred in Cleveland, Ohio, in 1969 when the Cuyahoga River became so laden with industrial waste that the river itself caught fire and the local fire department had to be called in to quench the flames! It appears that the creed of society in those years might have been to "subdue the earth, the earth is solely for our use and enjoyment." Indeed, "resource stewardship" was not commonly understood or even considered. Fortunately, that was beginning to change. Activities, many initiated by private organizations and individuals, helped federal and state agencies move forward with conservation agendas.

Major efforts to stem the tide of irresponsible use of natural resources began under the leadership of President Theodore Roosevelt, who established the U.S. Forest Service in 1905. In 1916, Congress acted to establish our National Park Service and later passed the landmark Wilderness Act in 1964, and in 1968, the National Wild and Scenic Rivers Act. Later, Congress appropriated money to help the states protect local natural areas; these funds were intended to be available on a recurring basis but were diverted under later administrations. Recognizing the need for government to assume a continuing responsibility for protecting the health of our environment and in an effort to reduce air and water pollution, Congress passed the Clean Air Act in 1970 and the Clean Water Act in 1977. The Department of Agriculture's Natural Resources Conservation Service, then Soil Conservation Service, was created in the 1930s to help landowners conserve soil and other natural resources, and has been a major contributor to sound resource planning over the years. And, very important, state agencies were created to develop and manage fish and wildlife resources and parks. Over the years, the functions of these resource agencies have expanded to include protection of air and water quality, rare species, and outdoor recreational activities. Gradually, environmental stewardship has woven its way into the fabric of our national consciousness, and we can look forward to an increasingly sophisticated attitude of enlightenment toward the protection of our natural resources.

While the role of government agencies in resource stewardship is relatively well known to the public, the role of private corporations is less well known. This book describes the exemplary role that Duke Power, now a business unit of Duke Energy Corporation, has played in helping preserve important conservation lands in the mountains, foothills, and piedmont regions of the Carolinas. It is the story of a major, publicly held utility corporation, successfully serving its employees, customers, and shareholders while, at the same time, working cooperatively with

agencies and conservation organizations to demonstrate resource stewardship through land conservation. The result of Duke Power's approach to land conservation has provided long-lasting benefits to the protection of our regional natural resources and, consequently, to the people who enjoy them.

SOME HISTORY OF DUKE POWER

One hundred years ago the South was struggling to recover from the ravages of the Civil War. Cotton farming was the dominant way of life. The landscape looked very different from the one we know today. Rather than the patchwork of forest, pasture, and development we now see, open fields and farm operations prevailed. Eventually, the combination of the dreaded boll weevil and abusive agricultural practices caused severe erosion and gradually many farms were abandoned.

It was during this period—1905 to 1930—that Duke Power Company began to furnish electricity to the public and to operate electric rail transportation systems in the Carolinas. Duke acquired thousands of acres of land in the mountains and built hydroelectric facilities to harness the power of rivers racing down from the Blue Ridge Mountains.

During the process of acquiring lands for the hydro projects, Duke encountered many farmers eager to dispose of their marginal or abandoned farmlands. In some instances, this resulted in Duke's purchasing land that was not actually required for its projects. Duke soon found an excellent use for these properties. By the 1930s, a new and revolutionary type of "farming" had evolved—tree farming. Newly discovered chemical processes made it possible to convert pine tree pulp into useful forms of paper. Prior to this discovery, only hardwoods, largely from northern forests, were used extensively for pulp. This new technology radically changed land use in the piedmont and throughout the South. It was a change that brought positive results for southern lands. Row crops that had

The Oconee Bell, common in the Toxaway Game Land

required annual harvesting and tilling with consequent soil erosion were gradually replaced with a crop that was harvested about every fifteen years. Tilling the soil was no longer necessary. Duke initiated tree farming on its holdings during the late 1930s and soon formed a Timber Management Division to plant and manage these forestlands.

In the 1960s Duke also acquired major tracts for future hydroelectric sites along headwater tributaries of the Savannah River. The rivers in these properties—the Thompson, Horsepasture, Keowee, Whitewater, and Toxaway—flow across the North Carolina-South Carolina border in an area known as the Blue Ridge Escarpment. To manage its forests and other natural resources, Duke created a subsidiary, Crescent Land & Timber Corporation.

In addition to managing these lands for forest products, Crescent actively partnered in other conservation efforts. For example, for many years Crescent leased extensive areas to state agencies for public game land programs. The company also participated in wildlife research programs that have included studies of black bear populations, trout stream surveys, rare species preservation, and trout habitat enhancement.

In 1997, Duke Energy was born when Duke Power and PanEnergy Corporation completed their merger. Today, Duke Power and Crescent Resources, LLC are separate business units of Duke Energy. Duke Power provides electricity to more than two million customers in North Carolina and South Carolina. Crescent Resources focuses on land management and real estate development throughout the southeastern and southwestern United States.

Duke Power's management philosophy has been attuned to improving the quality of life in the Carolinas. Its officers and directors understood the fabric of life of the various communities and the quality of life the citizens desired. They recognized the overriding importance of good environmental quality. At the same time, the leaders of Duke Power, over all of these decades, were fully cognizant of their responsibilities to the Company's customers and shareholders.

By balancing all of these issues Duke Power and Duke Energy Corporation earned impressive recognition in both the corporate and environmental worlds over the past decades. A few examples: In 1972, 1984, and 1995, Duke won the Edison Award, the electric utility industry's highest honor. Duke is the only utility to win this award three times. In 1998, 1999, and 2000, *Fortune* magazine named Duke Energy Corporation, the parent company of Duke Power, as the Most Admired Gas and Electric Utility. In the same years, Duke Energy Corporation was named by the *Financial Times* of London as the World's Most Respected Utility.

In the environmental field, Duke has received more than forty-five citations and awards for outstanding achievements in environmental protection and natural resource conservation. These include recognition from the Environmental Protection Agency in 1996 for outstanding risk-minimization practices in the use of herbicides. That same year, the National Arbor Day Foundation spotlighted Duke for its right-of-way maintenance activities. Duke also received an award from the Soil and Water Conservation Society of America for controlling erosion and protecting water quality while constructing the Bad Creek Pumped Storage Station. In 2001 the National Wildlife Federation awarded Duke Energy Corporation its Leadership Award for Outstanding Conservation Achievement. Both South Carolina and North Carolina have recognized Duke Power numerous times for its exemplary work in the field of conservation.

But Duke has not only managed its lands well, it has donated, or made available for sale to public agencies, many special places. These efforts began as far back as 1962, when Duke donated to the North Carolina park system 1,400 acres on the

Mountain Laurel blossoms

shore of Lake Norman. Today these lands form Lake Norman State Park. Some years later, the Company gave more than 200 acres to the South Carolina state park system that formed the nucleus of the Landsford Canal State Park. Since then, Duke has moved more than 7,300 acres of waterfront property in the Catawba River watershed to state or county resource agencies.

Duke continued taking an active environmental and conservation stance throughout the 1970s. As the nuclear facilities at Lake Keowee and Lake Jocassee's pumped storage facility were under construction, the Company recognized the extraordinary quality of its large contiguous holdings in these areas. Of course, Duke considered the lands, which had been acquired and thoughtfully managed over the decades, as a major company asset for core business activities and other potential development. To help analyze how these properties should be handled, Duke created an internal Land Use Committee. Its charge was to identify the lands needed for the company's long-range business needs at Jocassee and, at the same time, give thoughtful consideration to ways to permanently protect such extraordinary natural resources. The Land Use Committee also began to consider other Duke holdings throughout the Carolinas with those objectives in mind.

The Committee divided the lands into categories based on evaluations of future power generation and development. At the same time, the Committee recognized fragile areas, areas of outstanding beauty, and the location of rare species. Following the Committee's recommendations, Duke restricted activities where a rare species might

need protection or set aside buffers to protect streams. If, in these processes, the Company decided to divest itself of any of these quality natural or cultural resource lands, Duke consistently offered to sell the tracts first to state or federal resource agencies or to private conservation agencies.

As a result of the Company's generosity, the total acreage of protected lands now equals 69,000 acres! This book attempts to capture the twenty-one special places comprising this vast acreage in six chapters.

I extend my heartfelt thanks to several Duke Power employees: John Garton for his patience in leading me around the special places in North Carolina, Robert Siler for also helping to not only recount the history of each place but also showing me the rich diversity of plant and animal life; and Jennifer Huff who kept us on schedule.

It has been a very rewarding experience spending time in the field and attempting to grasp these varied "special places;" it has been both a strenuous exercise and a fabulous opportunity. It has been a special privilege for me to produce this book because I deeply admire and appreciate what Duke Power has accomplished for the cause of conservation over the past forty years. This book represents an effort to document those accomplishments for posterity. Not only has Duke Power been an outstanding corporate leader by any standard, but, at the same time, it has left an extraordinary legacy. This combination of business and conservation success sets an example and should provide an inspiration to other corporate leaders.
            —*Thomas Wyche*

Above, Mayapple and Jack-in-the-Pulpit
Opposite, Strange embrace of roots

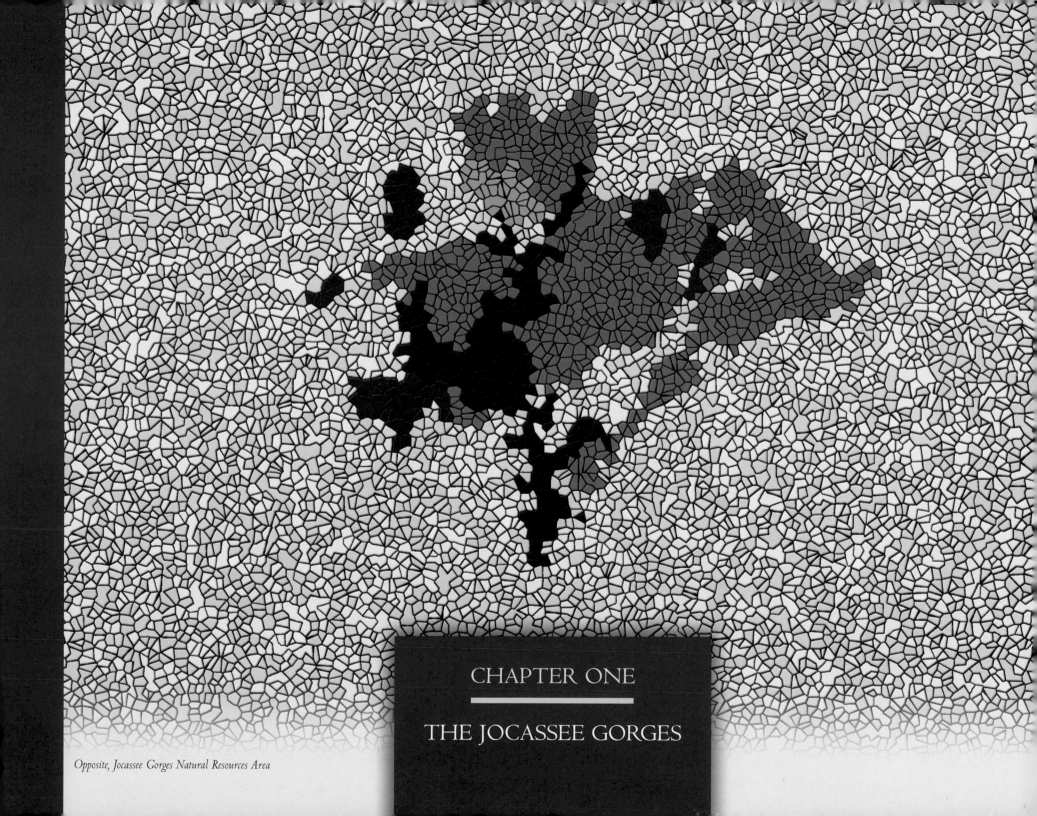

CHAPTER ONE

THE JOCASSEE GORGES

Opposite, Jocassee Gorges Natural Resources Area

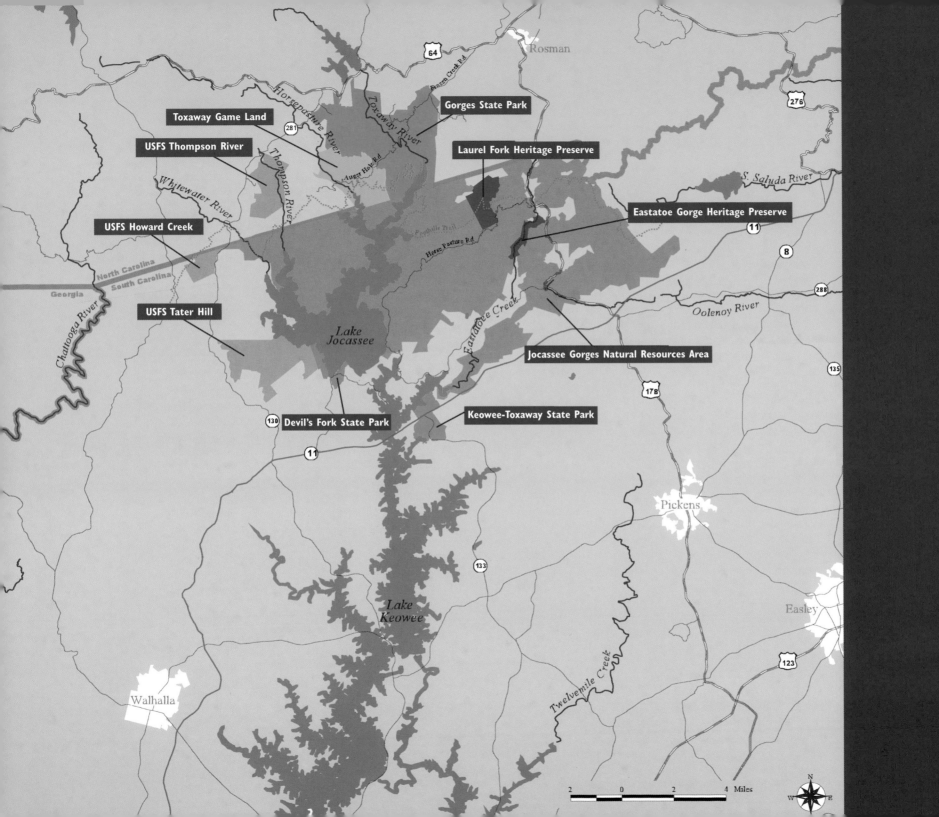

Toxaway Game Land

Gorges State Park

USFS Thompson River

Laurel Fork Heritage Preserve

USFS Howard Creek

Eastatoe Gorge Heritage Preserve

USFS Tater Hill

Jocassee Gorges Natural Resources Area

Devil's Fork State Park

Keowee-Toxaway State Park

Horsepasture River

Toxaway River

Frozen Creek Rd

Whitewater River

Thompson River

Auger Hole Rd

Foothills Trail

Horse Pasture Rd

S. Saluda River

Eastatoe Creek

Oolenoy River

Chattooga River

North Carolina

South Carolina

Georgia

Lake Jocassee

Lake Keowee

Twelvemile Creek

Rosman

Pickens

Easley

Walhalla

64

281

276

11

8

288

135

178

130

11

133

123

2   0   2   4 Miles

NINE SEPARATE AREAS comprise the parks, wildlife management areas, and preserves of Jocassee Gorges, as this area on the North Carolina-South Carolina border has come to be known. Seven of the areas, about 39,000 acres, are in South Carolina, and three, about 11,000 acres, are in North Carolina.

Superlatives cannot be avoided when describing this spectacular wilderness of nearly 50,000 acres of mountain lands, cut by steep ravines, rushing streams, and scores of waterfalls, and abundant plant and animal life. These wilderness properties, once owned by Duke, are now owned and managed by agencies of the states of North Carolina and South Carolina and the U.S. Forest Service. In the heart of the wilderness lies Lake Jocassee, a 7,500-acre turquoise jewel of clear, pure water of remarkable beauty. Duke continues to own and operate this lake as part of its hydroelectric pumped storage complex.

Jocassee Gorges is one of the most biologically diverse and important landscapes in the eastern United States. This extraordinary wilderness resource, standing alone, was a compelling cause for preservation. But the Jocassee Gorges does not stand alone. Like the keystone of a great arch, this 50,000-acre tract links two other large natural preserves of the Blue Ridge Escarpment to form a 167,000-acre unspoiled natural area. On the east, South Carolina's Table Rock State Park and the Mountain Bridge Wilderness encompass some 47,000 acres; and on the west, more than 70,000 acres of Sumter, Nantahala, and Chatahoochee National Forests, stretch along the Blue Ridge Escarpment. Together,

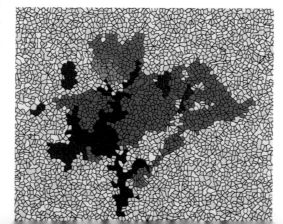

these lands comprise a wilderness area of truly national significance—especially important today in view of the fact that it is located within one of the fastest growing regions in the country.

Recorded history of this part of what are now the Carolinas dates back to the explorations by De Soto in 1589 in the vicinity of the Keowee River. The capital of the Lower Cherokee Indian Nation was located on the Keowee at Keowee Town, a short distance downstream from where the Jocassee Dam now stands. The Keowee flows through Oconee County and the county's name derives from Uk-Oo-Na, meaning "watery eyes of the hills," doubtless referring to the myriad springs, streams and creeks of the Blue Ridge Escarpment. The Cherokee called the escarpment the Blue Wall, an apt phrase for the nearly vertical mountainsides that rise more than 4,000 vertical feet within three or four miles.

By the late 1700s trade routes between the Cherokees and the English had become well established, with Keowee Town the hub along the trading path that extended into Tennessee. Eventually, relations between the Indians and the English became tense and hostilities erupted. The Governor of South Carolina had Fort Prince George constructed on the bank of the Keowee opposite the Indian capital.

A war ensued; in November 1785, at a meeting on the banks of the Keowee, Indian chiefs signed a treaty with General Andrew Pickens, surrendering all of what is now the area of the Jocassee Gorges to the United States.

The Cherokee called the area Jocassee, which means "Place of the Lost One," a phrase derived from

a legend of a princess named Jocassee whose lover was killed in a tribal battle by her brother. Upon seeing the severed head of her lover, the princess slipped away in a canoe; she then stepped into the river, but instead of sinking, she walked across it to meet the ghost of her lover and disappeared.

The fertile valleys of the Horsepasture, Laurel Fork, Toxaway and Eastatoe Rivers attracted greater and greater numbers of European settlers, even while the land was under Indian control. Land grants in this area were recorded as early as 1791.

Horsepasture became a common name used by settlers for the Jocassee area during the Civil War. When word spread that Sherman and his troops were on their way into upper South Carolina on their march from Savannah, the settlers, whose livelihood depended on their livestock, herded their animals into this "pasture for horses," to hide them in this remote, secluded valley. The rugged terrain provided a natural barrier to Sherman's advance. Unfortunately, the valley was inundated in August 1916, when the dam on Lake Toxaway broke, flooding out residents and depositing a three-foot layer of sand in the once fertile vale.

In addition to fur trading and agriculture, the Jocassee Gorges incubated an industry new to the mountains. In the early 1900s logging virgin timber emerged as a major source of employment. Various timber companies were formed, a sawmill was built in Pickens, South Carolina, and the Pickens Railroad became an important link to the Southern Railway for loggers. By 1927, however, timber had to be cut in increasingly remote and steep mountains, and hauling it out by horse and mule-drawn wagons was no longer practicable. The easy days of timber harvesting had passed.

In January 1927, three New York capitalists formed the Appalachian Lumber Company, a New York corporation, and easily raised $1.6 million with a stock offering. (This equates to approximately $10 million adjusted for inflation today!) With these funds, the Company constructed a huge, triple-band sawmill near Pickens large enough to handle trees sixty inches in diameter. It then purchased the Pickens Railroad and built logging railroads and spurs along the creeks, with

Opposite, Sunset and wake of lone boat at Jocassee
Right, Sluice of racing white water on Cane Creek in the Jocassee Gorges

trestles spanning deep ravines to reach the most remote areas where the "big 'uns" grew.

It didn't take long for the New Yorkers to learn about the basic religious nature of Southerners. At first, the Appalachian Lumber Company conducted its logging operations every day of the week in spite of the local custom to observe the Sabbath as a day of rest. One particular Sunday, an engine broke down, and the problems they met to restore it to service were so severe that the Company never again operated on Sundays.

Appalachian Lumber Company went bankrupt in June 1929 due, in part, to a torrential rainstorm that washed out many of the train trestles. Logging in the remote mountain areas came to an abrupt halt. Today, as you walk along the abandoned railroad beds, you frequently come upon rails, sometimes partly buried, sometimes partly spanning a creek where the rail is bent like a pretzel from the force of the rain-swollen stream. And, you can't help but be amazed at the engineering and construction feats of excavation, achieving a constant grade, building the trestles over deep ravines, and bringing in the rails themselves, all in extremely remote and mountainous terrain.

Many years after the rail logging operations were abandoned, the rails were salvaged, hauled out of the mountains, and sold for scrap. During World War II, George Bowie, Jr., who grew up here, was serving as soldier in the military occupation of a Japanese island and came upon a piece of rail which had "Pickens Railroad" molded on its side!

Duke Power Company's involvement in the area began in 1913 when Duke realized the hydroelectric potential of Lower Whitewater Falls. It purchased 400 acres along this stretch of the Whitewater River and made additional purchases over the decades until the Company had acquired some 65,000 acres in the area. Duke's subsidiary, Crescent Land & Timber Corporation, as it was then known, took over management of the non-utility portion of these lands. Crescent produced forest products and also implemented reforestation; it set aside the first "natural

Cane Creek waterfall

area" for preservation and registered the lands into South Carolina's and North Carolina's Wildlife Management Area programs to provide public access for hunting and fishing.

In 1966 Duke began construction of Oconee Nuclear Station (2,600-mw), one of the most successful nuclear energy plants in the nation. This required damming the Keowee River to create the 18,000-acre Lake Keowee. Above this lake, Duke developed a second lake, Lake Jocassee, to serve the 610-mw Jocassee Pumped Storage Hydro Station. The 1,200-mw Bad Creek Pumped Storage Station was completed at the upper end of Lake Jocassee in 1991. These are among the largest pumped storage operations in the country. Together, Jocassee and Bad Creek have the capacity to generate at any one time more than 1.8 million kilowatts! To put the magnitude of these facilities in some perspective, Duke's original hydro-electric plant, built in 1905, produced 6,600 kilowatts.

Duke's Internal Land Use Planning Committee continued to help shape not only Duke's business strategies, but its conservation programs as well. The Committee and Duke recognized the importance of the Jocassee Gorges and their unique physical and wildlife resources. The Company concluded that the lands were so outstanding and important that it would be appropriate to give the conservation community—both state and federal agencies—the first opportunity to acquire the property.

This decision was received with great excitement throughout the region in both South Carolina and North Carolina. Even though there was broad support for the project, the acquisition of these lands was complicated and took several years to conclude. The purchase of the South Carolina lands would not have been possible without the very generous financial support of the Richard K. Mellon Foundation working closely with The Conservation Fund. Duke's generosity in selling the property at substantially less than its true value was also a critical factor.

A piece of the Blue Ridge Escarpment

JIM TIMMERMAN NATURAL RESOURCES AREA

The Jim Timmerman Natural Resources Area (at Jocassee Gorges), managed by South Carolina's Department of Natural Resources, is one of the largest single properties held by a state agency in South Carolina. With 32,000 acres of forests, clear streams, waterfalls, and abundant wildlife, the property borders a considerable portion of the shoreline of Lake Jocassee. The tract, located in Pickens County, contains some of the highest mountain peaks and ridges in the state, with elevations rising to more than 3,000 feet, as well as some of the most forested and remote mountain coves. Brown and rainbow trout thrive in the tract's streams; springtime wildflowers bloom in abundance, and rare ferns, lichens, and mosses grow here. The endemic Oconee Bell is found along the lake's shoreline and within the property. Stands of mature forests provide habitat for songbirds, and the area contains the healthiest black bear population in the southern Appalachian Mountains.

There are many ways to enjoy this wonderland. You may launch your boat to explore Lake Jocassee at Devil's Fork State Park. Several beautiful waterfalls—Laurel Fork and Mills Creek, for example—drop straight into the lake. You can beach your boat near the Foothill Trails Bridge that spans the Horsepasture River or at the suspension bridge over the Toxaway River. From these landings and at other designated locations, you can access the eighty-mile Foothills Trail built in 1980; Duke built approximately half of the trail which traverses much of the Gorges and can provide days of true wilderness hiking and camping.

The Horsepasture, Thompson, and other rivers, may be reached by boat or from the trail, and they are a fisherman's dream where brown and rainbow trout abound. The lucky angler may even catch a native brook trout. Deeper in the interior, beautiful waterfalls tumble into nearly every stream, and in many places the rugged ravines offer challenges for those who want to tread where no one else has dared to go. For biologists, Jocassee Gorges sustains a remarkable wildlife habitat, one of the most remarkable ecosystems in the United States. The high annual rainfall, averaging ninety inches per year, and the high elevations and shaded ravines contribute to a complex assemblage of flora that includes plants from tropical and boreal types.

The Jim Timmerman Natural Resources Area is named for Dr. Jim Timmerman, retired Director of the South Carolina Department of Natural Resources, in recognition of his vital role in initiating and successfully pursuing the partnership with Duke Power and Crescent Resources, Inc. that resulted in the successful acquisition of this large part of Jocassee Gorges for the State of South Carolina.

The State Department of Natural Resources manages the area. Call the Clemson office (864) 654-1671 for further information about the preserve. The preserve is on the west side of US 178. Travel north on US 178; 10 miles from SC Hwy 11, cross the bridge over Eastatoe Creek, and turn immediately left onto an unpaved road; continue to the parking area. Another way to reach the area is through the Duke Power Bad Creek Facility off SC 130, 10 miles north of SC 11. Boating access is from Devil's Fork State Park.

Above, Green landmark on Foothills Trail

Opposite, Remnants of logging railroad bridge, Side-of-the-Mountain Creek in the Jocassee Gorges

DEVIL'S FORK STATE PARK

Devil's Fork State Park is nestled on 644 acres in the mountains of Oconee County, South Carolina. On the western shore of Lake Jocassee, it is a doorway to the Jocassee Gorges area. The park's centerpiece is Lake Jocassee, the beautiful 7,500-acre mountain reservoir constructed by Duke Power in 1973. Devil's Fork provides expansive views of the clear blue waters of the lake and of the surrounding landscapes that arise out of the Jocassee Gorges and to the more distant mountains of the Blue Ridge Escarpment.

The park, one of the most popular parks in the upstate, has more than 400,000 visitors each year. It offers a variety of outdoor experiences such as

Opposite, Family fun on Lake Jocassee

Above, Truly picturesque

Right, Casual, comfortable fishing from, and in, Lake Jocassee

sailing and water skiing, and even scuba diving in the lake's icy, clear waters. There are exceptional opportunities for hiking, fishing, and primitive camping. RV camping facilities are also available, and there is "boat-in" camping for canoeists or kayakers who come equipped with tents and camping gear. For those who prefer a more protected outdoor experience, there are modern, fully equipped villas for rent.

The only public boat access to Lake Jocassee is at Devil's Fork. The lake is especially popular with anglers seeking brown and rainbow trout and smallmouth bass. Waterfall enthusiasts can arrange a pontoon boat tour of the lake and the cascades of its tributary waterfalls by contacting local private concessionaires.

Devil's Fork provides easy access for viewing the Oconee Bell. The natural range of this beautiful wildflower is largely restricted to the Lake Jocassee watershed,

and the mile-long Oconee Bell Nature Trail provides a good opportunity to observe this species in its native habitat. This trail is especially popular in mid to late March when Oconee Bells are at their peak. Some enthusiasts make an annual pilgrimage to Devil's Fork to see the Oconee Bell in flower and to welcome the start of another spring season in the South Carolina mountains.

Devil's Fork is managed by the South Carolina Department of Parks, Recreation and Tourism. For additional park information, call the Devil's Fork office at (864) 944-2649. To reach the park take SC 11. Traveling west on this road, turn right (north) onto Boone Creek Road (SC 25) after crossing a long bridge over an upper reach of Lake Keowee, and follow signs to the park.

Above left, Villas and Mountain Laurel on the lakeshore
Above right, The end of a perfect day

Eastatoe Creek Heritage Preserve

In 1979, the 375-acre Eastatoe Creek Heritage Preserve in Pickens County became one of the first areas set aside as part of South Carolina's Heritage Trust Program. Now more than fifty preserves make up this system, but Eastatoe Creek remains one of its gems.

Eastatoe Creek flows within a gorge from an elevation of around 1,400 feet to 1,200 feet. Ridges rise several hundred feet high above the creek. Hiking provides the only way to fully experience the rugged majesty of the gorge. There are huge trees, the crystal clear stream with deep swimming holes, and perfect tent sites located in a surprisingly large flat area on the creek's banks. This area is large enough to accommodate several groups. Downstream only a short distance from the entry

Above, Idyllic fishing in Eastatoe Creek
Right, The Eastatoe Narrows

point is a remarkable feature: the stream enters the Narrows, where the entire flow of the creek passes through a five-foot-wide channel in bedrock. Here, the Eastatoe enters a canyon some thirty feet deep, and as the water emerges from the Narrows, it plummets into a broad deep pool.

The steep gorge, with an annual average rainfall of ninety inches, creates a shady and moist habitat. Christmas fern, lady fern, hay-scented fern, maidenhair fern, rock cap fern, and other spore-bearing plants carpet the ground and hang from dripping rock faces. Two species of filmy ferns, known nowhere else in North America, occur on the Eastatoe.

The preserve's forest includes large hemlocks, white pine, Fraser's magnolia, and sweet birch. Scarlet oaks grow along the upper slopes, and white and red oaks occupy the lower slopes of the gorge. The Eastatoe is habitat for wild trout, and it is one of the premier trout streams in South Carolina—special fishing regulations apply to this stretch of the creek. There are also ruffed grouse and black bears, but it is the spectacular variety of plant species and the geography of the gorge itself that make the area unique.

The South Carolina Department of Natural Resources manages the area. For information call the Clemson office at (864) 654-6738 or (803) 734-3894. To reach the preserve, take US 178 north 10 miles from its intersection with SC 11, cross the bridge over Eastatoe Creek; turn immediately left onto unpaved road. Continue to a parking area and follow signs to Eastatoe Gorge.

Above left, Lone blossom on small cascade
Above right, Rhododendron blossoms "rain"
Opposite, In the Eastatoe Gorge

LAUREL FORK HERITAGE PRESERVE

This 1,000-acre South Carolina preserve features deep woods, a mountain stream with waterfalls, an excellent wild rainbow trout population, and a rich variety of plant and other animal species. Laurel Fork Heritage Preserve takes its name from the meandering Laurel Fork Creek, and it is noted for its wildflower, fern, and amphibian communities. A short walk along the Foothills Trail in the preserve takes the hiker to outstanding examples of the natural resources of the Jocassee

Above, Humble beginnings for Laurel Fork Creek
Left, The final drop of Laurel Fork Creek Falls

Gorges area. These include wildflower displays of trilliums, jack-in-the pulpit, showy orchis, wood lilies, bloodroot, long-spurred violets, bellwort, trailing arbutus, black cohosh, wood anemones, and other showy species. There is only a small population of Oconee Bells in the preserve, but farther downstream on Laurel Fork—outside of the preserve—there is an abundance of the flowers. There are also lush growths of fern species including cinnamon fern, lady fern, maidenhair fern, Christmas fern, rattlesnake fern, and rock cap fern.

Laurel Fork Creek and other nearby streams and seepage areas provide quality habitat for many rare amphibians. Species of salamanders found here include the blackbelly, dusky, spring, Appalachian woodland, red, two-lined, slimy, seal, and green salamanders, among others.

The South Carolina Department of Natural Resources manages the area. For information call the Clemson office at (864) 654-6378. To reach the area, take US 178 north; 10 miles from its intersection with SC 11 cross the bridge over Eastatoe Creek; turn immediately left onto unpaved road and continue to the parking lot. The Foothills Trail may be accessed at this parking lot and followed for several miles. Or vehicles are permitted past the parking area on the unpaved road to a gate at Laurel Fork (approximately 5 miles). From that gate hikers may follow a short trail down to an old closed roadbed and follow it along Laurel Fork Creek about 0.5 mile. No reservations or permits are necessary.

Above, An unusual large fungus
Right, Foothills Trail climbing to Laurel Fork Heritage Preserve

KEOWEE–TOXAWAY STATE PARK

South Carolina's Keowee-Toxaway State Park, 1000 acres, has beautiful hardwood and mixed pine forests, major geologic formations, and beautiful natural settings. Many of these features can be experienced by hiking the nature trails that begin at the parking area just north of SC 11. The Natural Bridge Trail is a one-mile loop that takes the hiker along Poe Creek with its small waterfalls, splash pools, and open forest settings. In early spring, this trail offers many blooming wildflowers, including trout lily, faded trillium, green and gold, blazing star and others. Colonies of Allegheny spurge, a rare South Carolina wildflower that grows only in a few locations in the entire state can be found along this trail.

The Raven Rock Hiking Trail leads hikers another two miles into the backcountry of Keowee-Toxaway, where there are large and scenic rock domes and other extensive outcrops. These are areas of special interest and beauty, and many of them provide vistas of the surrounding landscapes. Several backcountry campsites are

Above, History and guidance for the visitors
Left, A lovely trail in the Keowee-Toxaway

available for primitive camping along this trail. The park also features informational displays about the Cherokee who once lived in the Keowee River area through a series of kiosks located along a 0.25-mile walking trail; visitors may also buy books on local Native American history in the park office.

A stay at the park's campground may reward visitors with an opportunity to see white-tailed deer, a flock of wild turkeys, or other wildlife that abounds in the forests, streams, and lakeside areas. The park maintains one large rental cabin that overlooks Lake Keowee.

For information, call the park office at (864) 868- 2605. The area is managed by the South Carolina Department of Parks, Recreation and Tourism. The park is a short distance from SC 11's intersection with SC 133. The main entrance to the park's headquarters and visitors center is on the south side of SC 11. There are also picnic areas and interpretive walking trails at that entrance. The park entrance on the north side of SC 11 is the access to Lake Keowee; parking is not permitted near the lake. There are more hiking trails here.

Above, An old church for the mountain folk—now a public meeting place
Right, Seepage of water and the beginning of a mountain stream

Howard Creek and Tater Hill, Sumter National Forest

These tracts, totaling 4,000 acres, are major additions to Sumter National Forest in northwestern South Carolina. The northern tract, along upper Howard Creek, contains areas of deep cove forest habitats. This natural forest gives the visitor an immediate sense of a wilderness of immense calm. There are no designated trails, only animal trails. Such tracks may lead into dense cathedrals of conifers underlain by verdant ferns. The towering pines are like ranks of straight-backed soldiers, which bend in lazy synchronization with the wind. Here the trunks and stumps of trees wear dense coats of lichens. Clouds cast fleeting gray shadows that block for an instant the sun that highlights a billion green-black fingers of needles and leaves. The setting offers stillness found only in mature natural forests.

A small stream, Howard Creek, cavorts through a jumble of fallen limbs and moss stained boulders. This is a place of thickly tangled rhododendron and dense thickets of mountain laurel. It is also the habitat of Leucothoe, or dog-hobble, named because dogs, chasing bears, were led into and hobbled by these plants. The creek slides sinuously over long, flat granite slabs, creating a child's sliding-rock paradise.

Howard Creek has waterfalls and cascades, and rainbow trout flourish throughout most of its length. The upper two miles of this creek and some of its tributaries also support wild brook trout. In addition to steep gradient sections with waterfalls and cascades, the watershed has flat valleys populated by beaver colonies.

The southern tract includes the headwaters of Corbin Creek, another stream supporting wild brown and rainbow trout. One section of Corbin flows through a flat open valley surrounded by wooded hillsides and beautiful mountain coves. Rolling foothills and flat valleys provide excellent wildlife habitat for wild turkeys, wood ducks, and ruffed grouse. Trout fisherman and hunters are the primary users of the area.

The Tater Hill area, also in the southern tract, is a favorite among hunters. Select portions here have been intensively managed for game and non-game

Left, Dense shade, frequent rain: ideal habitat for ferns
Opposite, Howard Creek slowly gains size and strength

Above, Corbin Creek flows through the ferns in Tater Hill

Opposite, Beaver dam covered in Jewel Weed

wildlife through timber management and wildlife food plantings. Dry forest communities dominate the ridges of this area, while the endemic Southern Appalachian wildflower, Oconee Bells, occurs in the sheltered areas along the streams. Because portions of Tater Hill have not been timbered for many years, it is reverting to mature forest, offering rich opportunities for off-trail hiking, camping, and wilderness exploration.

To reach the northern tract, travel north from SC 11 on SC 130 to its intersection with SC 413 on the west. This tract lies on both sides of SC 413. To reach the southern, and much larger, tract, travel north from SC 11 about 5 miles on SC 130. This tract borders the eastern side of SC 130 for more than one mile. Both of these tracts are in the Andrew Pickens District of Sumter National Forest. For information call (864) 638-9568.

Jocassee Gorges

Above left, Haircap and Reindeer Moss
Above, Well along in the cycle of a mature forest
Opposite, A distant view of the rugged Jocassee Gorges

Gorges State Park

Established in 1999, Gorges State Park, just west of Sapphire, North Carolina, embraces more than 6,000 acres of mountainous terrain in Transylvania County. It is a true wilderness, characterized by massive landscapes, expansive unbroken

Above, A view from Upper Bearwallow Falls in Gorges State Park

Above right, At the foot of Upper Bearwallow Falls

Opposite, The Toxaway River—the longest stream in Gorges State Park

forests, and roaring rivers with high waterfalls. The Toxaway River and Bearwallow Creek are two major streams within the park. Over time these streams have cut deep gorges as they lost elevation from their headwaters at 3,000 feet down to 1,100 feet.

The gorges and mountain coves associated with the streams support many rare species of plants. Spring wildflower displays rival any in the Southern Appalachians. Wildlife abounds in the park. There are rainbow and brown trout in the streams, and bald eagles, black bears, peregrine falcons, and ruffed grouse flourish here. Many species of salamanders thrive due, in part, to the park's abundant streams, waterfalls and wet places.

Ten miles of the eighty-mile long Foothills Trail traverse the park, and hikers can gain access to it on trails and closed roadways within the park. One of these roads leads to the suspension bridge over the Toxaway River. It is the Trail's largest bridge and provides hikers with a stunning view of the river and headwaters of Lake Jocassee. There are other hikes that follow long, old logging roads such as the one along Augur Fork Creek. This old road eventually crosses the Toxaway. Several other hikes follow logging roads which branch off from Augur Fork Creek.

Bearwallow Creek has two beautiful waterfalls: one, Lower Bearwallow Falls, is a short distance from the confluence of Bearwallow Creek and the Toxaway River; however, it is not accessible by trail but only by arduous bushwhacking. The top of Upper Bearwallow Falls can be reached by a fairly easy hike and affords a panoramic view of the Gorges area; there is a steep path down to lower levels of two beautiful cascades.

While the park remains largely undeveloped, its size and diverse landscapes provide visitors the opportunity to escape into a large, untamed wilderness. North Carolina's Division of Parks and Recreation manages the park and maintains a temporary visitors center near Sapphire on US 64 near its junction with NC 281. For more information call (828) 966-9099. To reach the park, travel east on NC 281, a short distance after crossing the bridge over the Horsepasture River, you will see signs for the park on the right.

Jocassee Gorges

Above, Remnants of an early settler's home
Opposite, In the lower reaches of the Toxaway River

Toxaway Game Land

This 3,000-plus acre tract of game land in Transylvania County, North Carolina has an array of stunning cliffs hundreds of feet tall, huge rock formations, boulders, and plunging ravines. But the area's most breathtaking feature is, without question, the Horsepasture River and its gorge.

Left, The foaming whitewater of the Horsepasture River continues
to deepen this awesome gorge through Toxaway Game Land
Above, Monster boulders line the river banks
Opposite, An example of the sheer rock faces in Toxaway Game Land

The Toxaway Game Land offers hunting, fishing, and hiking opportunities in and along the Horsepasture Gorge. Steep-sided, massive, and incredibly beautiful, the gorge was carved over thousands of years by the Horsepasture River, the largest tributary to Lake Jocassee. Largely because of its loveliness and two stunning waterfalls—Rainbow and Windy—the lower four-mile stretch of the Horsepasture River has been classified as a National Wild and Scenic River. The section acquired from Duke begins at the top of Windy Falls and continues downstream to Lake Jocassee; this includes about half of the Wild and Scenic River stretch.

While the Horsepasture invites trout fishing, photography, and the simple enjoyment of a major mountain river, the surrounding game land provides a wild

Opposite, The Foothills Trail Bridge crosses the Horsepasture close to Lake Jocassee
Above, A camping group prepares for the evening
Right, A young vine clings to a young tree and together, for decades, they climb toward the sky

woodland setting. This rugged country is home to black bear, wild turkey, ruffed grouse, and many other species. Hunting is permitted, and primitive campsites are available during hunting season.

Mature forests of oak, hickory, Fraser's magnolia, American beech, hemlocks, white pine and pitch pine dominate the area. The hillsides, laced with mountain laurel, rhododendron, and many species of wildflowers, put on a flowery display in late spring.

The Toxaway Game Land is an area of extremes. It is extremely steep and in some sections, extremely difficult to access. It has extremely damp habitats, including those near seeps and in the spray zones of waterfalls. Yet these lands also contain extremely dry habitats in the upper gorge walls that are marked by spectacular outcroppings of bare rock. All of these areas contain specific plant communities that reflect these varied conditions.

The North Carolina Wildlife Resource Commission manages the area; for further information call (919) 733-7291. This game land can best be accessed from NC 281 through Gorges State Park. The Foothills Trail crosses into the game land at the bridge over the Horsepasture River.

THOMPSON RIVER, NANTAHALA NATIONAL FOREST

The 1,500-acre Thompson River tract in North Carolina is a recent addition to the Nantahala National Forest managed by the U.S. Forest Service. The tract's dominant feature is the Thompson River and its beautiful and wild river gorge. In only a few miles, the river cascades in giant waterfalls, deep pools and swiftly moving waters nearly 2,000 vertical feet, crossing into South Carolina before flowing into Lake Jocassee. The area offers world-class opportunities for trout fishing in a setting of truly extraordinary beauty.

Accessing the area can be a challenge because it is largely undeveloped, but hikers willing to accept the challenge of steep descents (and climbs back up!) of as much as 600 vertical feet are rewarded by a wild and verdant setting. The gorge slopes are thick with tall trees and rhododendrons. Giant boulders and rock

Left, A cluster of giant rocks by the Thompson River
Opposite, Misery Mountain, a steep border of the Thompson River

outcrops in the riverbed and lower slopes support dense growths of mosses and ferns. Forest coves beside the river nurture a diverse array of showy wildflowers, including several species of trillium, jack-in-the-pulpit, baneberry, Solomon seal, and showy orchis. Brown trout and rainbow trout occur in this section of the Thompson, and brook trout are in some tributary streams.

For additional information, call the Nantahala National Forest's Highlands Ranger District at (828) 526-3765. The tract is off of NC 281, near the North Carolina-South Carolina border where it crosses the Thompson River.

Above, Galax
Left, The Thompson River, one of four major tributaries to Lake Jocassee
Opposite, The Thompson River hurries on to Lake Jocassee

Opposite, The mountains which enclose Panthertown Valley

CHAPTER TWO

PANTHERTOWN VALLEY
NANTAHALA
NATIONAL FOREST

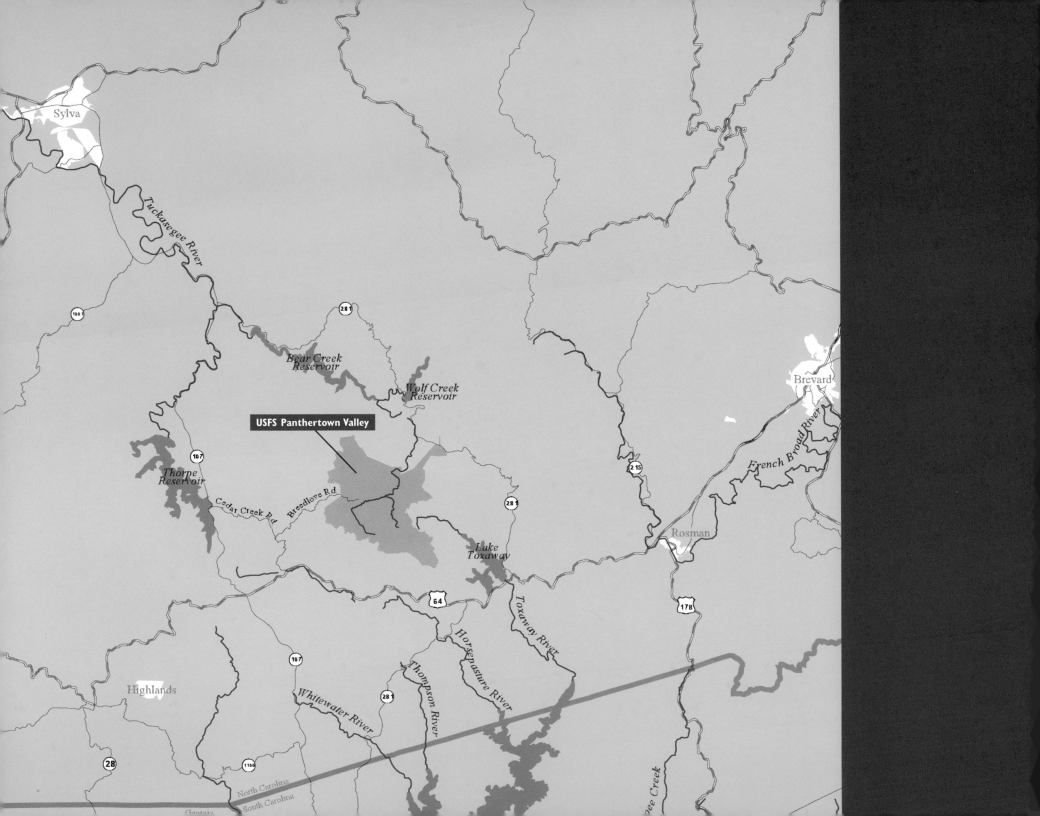

NORTH CAROLINA'S PANTHERTOWN VALLEY was once called Painter-town Valley, "painter" being another name for panther or mountain lion. Europeans began settling the valley in the 1800s. By 1920, a logging railroad had been built along the streams, and the valley was extensively logged over during the next decade. Evidence of railroad beds and anchors for tracks can still be found. Fires scorched the area in the 1930s leaving some ridges bare of vegetation, and erosion has exposed the granite domes that are visible throughout the area. Scenic vistas, especially from Salt Rock, led to the area being referred to as the "Yosemite of the East."

In the late 1970s and early 1980s the owner of Panthertown Valley had plans to develop the property with a lake in the valley and resort homes on the ridges. Fortunately, at that time, Duke was interested in constructing a transmission line to connect the Duke Power System with the Nantahala Power and Light Company system. In the mid-1980s Duke successfully negotiated purchasing 7,000 acres of the valley.

The National Park Service had long been interested in acquiring the property for a campground and recreation area. Duke identified and retained the land it needed for the transmission corridor and, with the aid of The Nature Conservancy, sold the remaining 6,700 acres to the U.S. Forest Service. Habitats found in the valley and the surrounding mountains and granite domes are now permanently protected.

Panthertown Valley, at an elevation of 3,600 feet, is surrounded by ridges soaring up to 4,760 feet.

While remote and not easy to get to, the area offers fantastic fishing, spectacular scenery, and showy wildflowers. There is no vehicle access into the tract, but there are more than fifty miles of hiking, horseback riding, and mountain biking trails. (The trails are not marked by the Forest Service.)

The valley is headwaters of the Tuckasegee River, formed by Panthertown and Greenland Creeks. Flat Creek, another major stream, and these waterways support thriving native brook trout populations. The darkly stained water of the valley may surprise a first time visitor who would not expect to see streams resembling coastal plain black-water streams. The black tint is the result of rainwater and seepages draining through organic matter that accumulates in the soil on the large areas of bedrock. In contrast, coarse white sands, eroded from the surrounding ridges, blanket the valley and most of the streambeds. Some of the slow moving streams have waterfalls such as Schoolhouse Falls on Greenland Creek and Granny Burrell's Pool located below a rockslide.

In addition to its special aquatic resources, Panthertown Valley is home to distinctive plant communities. The numerous granite domes and faces, the flat valleys of Frolictown and Panthertown Creek, and the bogs of Panthertown and Greenland Creek contain abundant wildflowers. The forested slopes support sprouting American chestnuts, spectacular flame azaleas with blooms varying from yellow to luminous red, and pink-shell azaleas. There are also impenetrable thickets of rosebay rhododendron along streams and near bogs, while painted trilliums

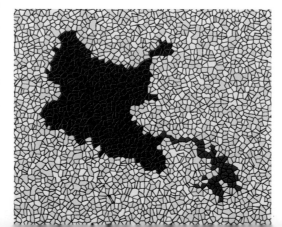

Above, White sand beaches contrast with the black water of Panthertown Creek

Opposite, Schoolhouse Falls formed by Greenland Creek

commonly grow in the shade of rhododendrons. Four other species of trillium also occur in the tract, and several areas contain large whorled *pogonia*.

The headwaters of Greenland Creek and portions of the Tuckasegee River lie near old growth stands of hemlock, black cherry, sweet birch, and red maple. Some trees in these forests are more than 250 years old.

nds
rest;
To
64
ock
go
oad
y 4

Above, A spacious campground on the banks of Panthertown Creek
Right, Hundreds of new frog eggs will soon emerge as a new crop
Opposite, The Tuckasegee River is born at the confluence of Panthertown Creek and Greenland Creek

45

Opposite, Kayaker on the Green River

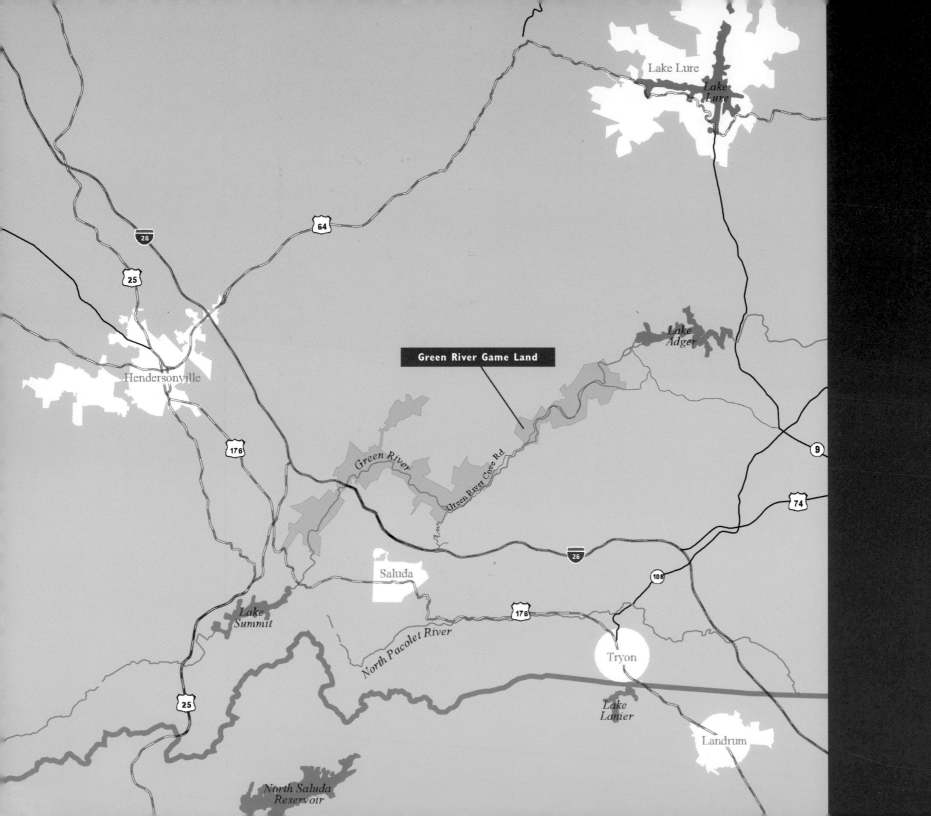

THE GREEN RIVER GAME LAND, in Polk and Henderson Counties, is a 12,000-acre tract of rugged, forested land along the Blue Ridge Escarpment, only a few miles from Saluda, North Carolina. Duke provided 5,000 of these acres through the cooperative efforts of The Nature Conservancy. The wild landscape of this tract is a blend of mountain and piedmont vegetation and a scenic, rugged river gorge with excellent populations of fish and wildlife. Recreational opportunities include trout fishing, hunting, hiking, canoeing, kayaking, and tubing.

The Green River drops 1,200 feet as it flows from Lake Summit to Lake Adger. Most of this drop occurs in a steep gorge in the upper parts of the river, including a stretch crossed by I-26. The topography is very steep, with waterfalls and dense forests that are difficult to access. Old growth stands grow on the gorge slopes, and the ground cover includes a rich variety of wildflowers. The Narrows in the gorge force the entire flow of the river through a ten-foot wide passage. This section is popular with kayakers, but it is extremely dangerous for even the most expert paddlers.

The Cove section of the river is downstream of the Gorge and flows along County Road 1151, which can be reached from Exit 28 on I-26 at Saluda. This part of the river is much more suitable for canoeing, tubing, and fishing.

Put-ins for canoeing are at two locations along County Road 1151. While the Cove section is less rugged than the Gorge, visitors can still enjoy deep pools, beautiful scenery, and waterfalls such as Bradley Falls.

For botanists, the Cove and Gorge sections provide an opportunity to observe more than 500 species of vascular plants. Here plant communities typical of the mountains and the piedmont grow in close proximity—truly a unique characteristic of the property.

Apart from acreage along the river, the Green River Game Land includes upland areas managed for both game and non-game wildlife. Visitors should take precautions during hunting season. Fifteen miles of hiking trails traverse the 12,000 acres, including trails in the spectacular Green River Gorge. These trails have been developed through a joint project involving the Henderson County-based Environmental and Conservation Organization and the North Carolina Wildlife Resources Commission. Hikers should not travel alone in this area because of its rugged and remote nature.

The North Carolina Wildlife Resources Commission manages the property; call (919) 733-7291 for more information. The most convenient access to the tract is from I-26, Exit 28 (for Saluda); take County Road 1151 north along river. The area can also be reached from Saluda.

Above, Boulders strewn like pebbles along the river

Opposite, A small tributary of the Green River

Above, Fire Pink flowers
Left, The beginning of a strenuous hike
Opposite, Old fashion fun in a deep pool
Below, All ages enjoy an exciting float on the river

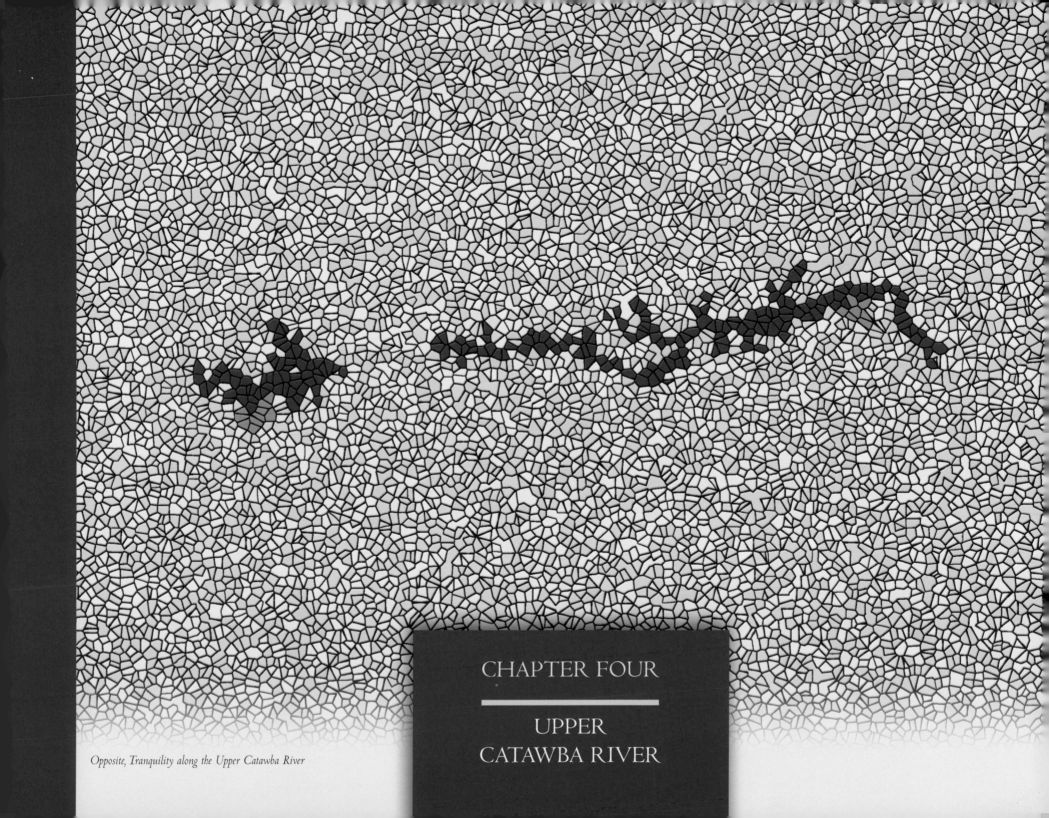

Opposite, Tranquility along the Upper Catawba River

CHAPTER FOUR

UPPER
CATAWBA RIVER

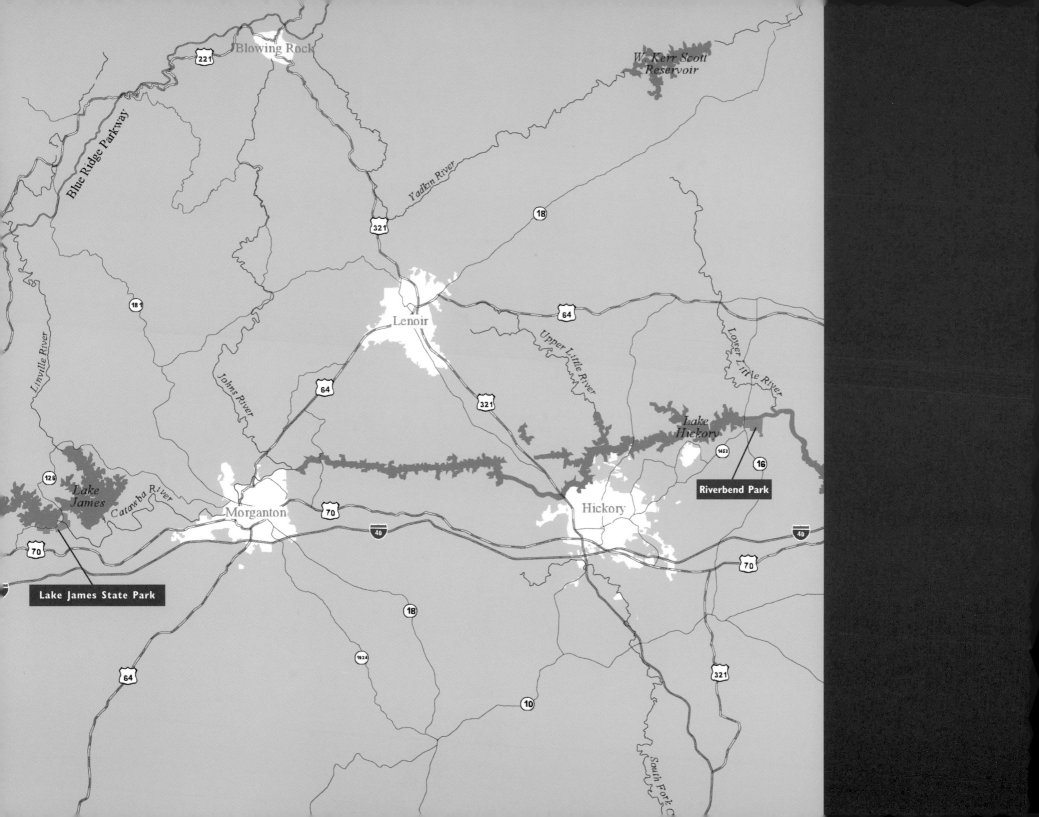

CATAWBA RIVER OVERVIEW

THE CATAWBA RIVER is the birthplace of Duke Power, or Southern Power, as the Company was called at the time of its beginnings in 1904. The company name was changed to Duke Power in the mid-1920s. Between 1904 and 1925, Duke constructed ten impoundments accompanied by twelve hydroelectric power stations on the river, whose headwaters are in the Blue Ridge of North Carolina. Those hydroelectric stations were the backbone of the electric generation system that enabled the arrival of industry to much of the piedmont region of the Carolinas in the early decades of the twentieth century. In the late 1950s Duke added the eleventh and largest reservoir, Lake Norman, impounded by Cowans Ford Dam. These reservoirs, in addition to providing hydroelectric generation, also provide the cooling water for Duke's highly efficient fossil and nuclear-fueled power plants that meet the base load electric generation demand of today's modern piedmont society. The lakes also offer drinking water for millions of residents in the river valley, water for sewage treatment, flood control, extensive public recreation, and real estate that is often highly desirable.

In addition to its reservoirs and generating facilities along the Catawba River, Duke has also provided lands for a group of parks and wildlife areas that form the core of public lands associated with the river. These lands may seem to many people to be a well kept secret, but they are certainly deserving of discovery. The areas provide opportunities for hiking, camping, fishing, and nature observation, and they protect rare species and unique cultural resources. They have fine wildflower glens, and provide nesting habitats for bald eagles, osprey, owls, hawks, and wading birds. They contain wetlands with many species of amphibians, piedmont prairies with unique associations of plants, environmental education facilities, and small streams with lots of critters. These are nearby wild places where people of the piedmont can escape for an afternoon or a weekend.

Presently, the lands for all state parks on the river (two in North Carolina and two in South Carolina), and a series of outstanding county parks and related conservation lands, have been provided by Duke. The parks range in size from 106-acre Jetton Park, a county park near Charlotte, to 1,400-acre Lake Norman State Park. There are three state parks on reservoirs—Lakes James, Norman, and Wateree—and Landsford Canal, which is on a free-flowing section of the Catawba. County-owned lands obtained from Duke include a series of parks and nature preserves up to 1,000 acres in size, a wildlife management area, and an educational forest.

Today, Duke continues to look for ways to work cooperatively with various resource agencies as they make long-range plans for public recreation opportunities along the Catawba River. These plans will include land conservation that can benefit people, wildlife, and the environment in this busiest and fastest growing region of the Carolinas.

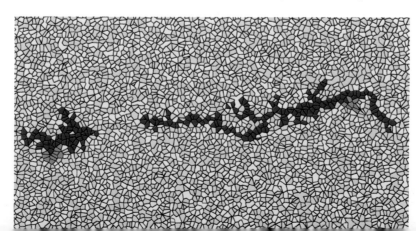

UPPER CATAWBA RIVER, LAKE JAMES STATE PARK

North Carolina's Lake James State Park, an area of approximately 600 acres, is located along the southern shore of Lake James, in Burke County. There are excellent views of the lake's clear mountain water and the surrounding Blue Ridge Mountains.

The park borders and serves as a jumping-off point for visiting other public lands in the area, including the Linville Gorge Wilderness Area in Pisgah National Forest. Lake James is a great destination for those who enjoy swimming, boating, fishing, camping, or bird-watching, and the park staff offer seasonal environmental programs about the lakeshore environment and its plant and animal life.

Lake James has excellent fishing for walleye, smallmouth bass, largemouth bass, and sunfish. The park's Hidden Cove and Canal Bridge boat launches offer access to the lake for powerboats and sailboats. Smaller craft can be launched for skiing, fishing or sightseeing. A number of nearby privately operated launch sites and marinas offer boats for rent for fishing and water skiing. Park concessions rent canoes from June 1 through Labor Day.

The park is primarily a day-use area, and closing times vary seasonally. Twenty backpack campsites are located 150 to 300 yards from the parking lot. Each campsite has a fireplace with a grill, a picnic table, and tent space; water and a washhouse are within a short walking distance. These campsites are available on a first-come basis March 15 through November 30 for a modest fee. Twenty picnic sites have tables, trash receptacles, and outdoor grills, with drinking water and restrooms nearby. A picnic shelter with twelve tables is available for group gatherings and is free, on a first-come, first-serve basis; there is a charge if a reservation is requested. Two hiking trails meander along the forested shoreline of Lake James to scenic vistas.

The North Carolina Division of Parks and Recreation manages the area. Call (828) 652-5047 for information. The Park is seven miles northeast of Marion. From I-40, take Exit 90, (Nebo/Lake James), drive north on NC 126, cross US 70, and follow signs to the park.

Above, Once every 17 years the locust emerges
Opposite, Families at play at Lake James State Park

The Upper Catawba River

Above, Spring is in the air

Opposite, A viewing platform at Riverbend Park

RIVERBEND PARK

Riverbend Park, in Catawba County, North Carolina, is a 450-acre county-managed park along the Catawba River. Established in 1999, it offers hiking, fishing, and boating activities. The park parallels the tailwater section of the Catawba River just downstream of the Oxford Dam on Lake Hickory. The entrance is off NC16 and provides access to park trails and a canoe and kayak launch site.

There is a network of hiking trails in the forests and fields that make up the Riverbend. One trail leads through the forested areas along the river, providing opportunities to view the river, access the river for fishing, and the opportunity to enjoy the abundant wildflowers that grow there. Another trail takes hikers, mountain bikers, and horseback riders through upland areas away from the river. There is also a pond, an alternative to fishing along the riverbanks.

Catawba County Parks manages Riverbend Park. For more information call (828) 256-9157.

Opposite, A gentle hike at Riverbend Park
Above, Seedpods of a Red Maple
Right, Foam Flower

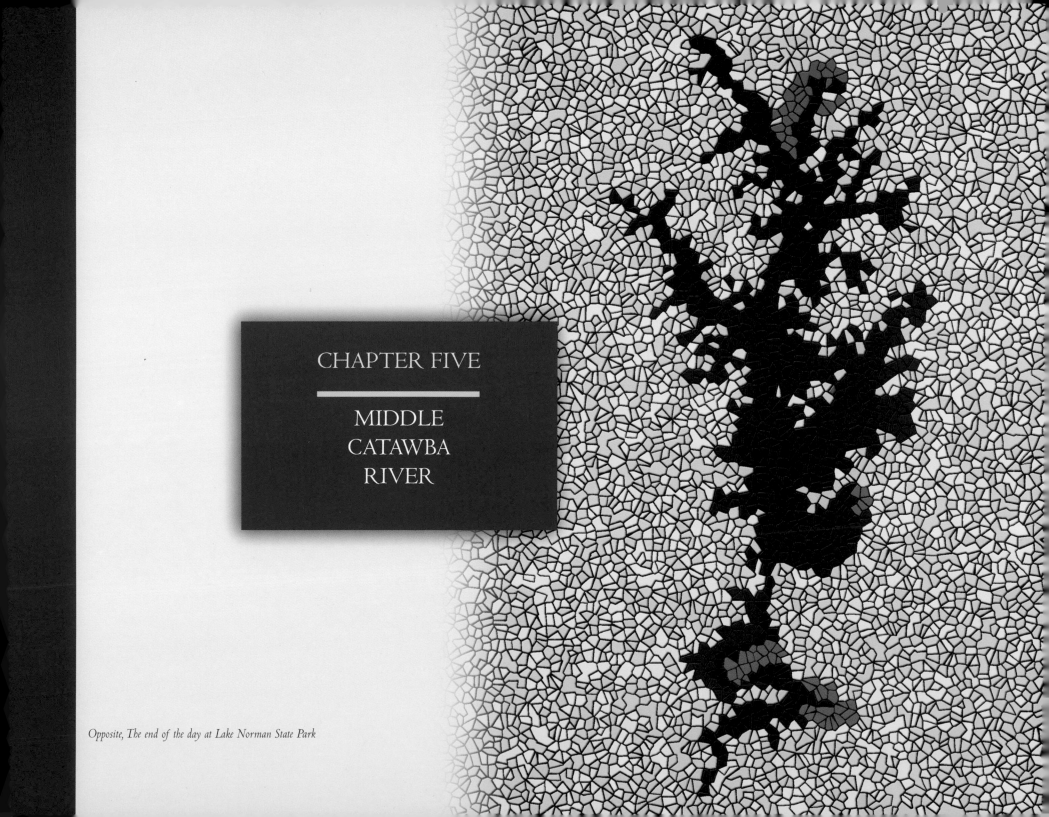

CHAPTER FIVE

MIDDLE CATAWBA RIVER

Opposite, The end of the day at Lake Norman State Park

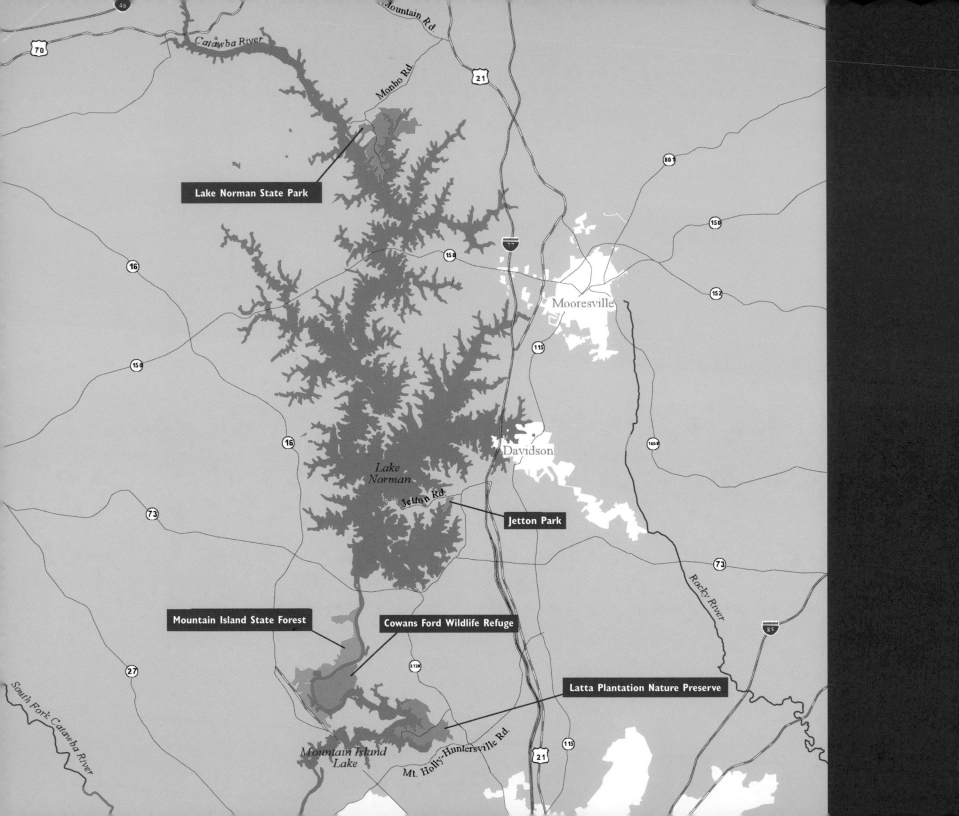

Lake Norman State Park

Catawba River

Monbo Rd

Mountain Rd

Mooresville

Davidson

Lake Norman

Jetton Rd.

Jetton Park

Mountain Island State Forest

Cowans Ford Wildlife Refuge

Latta Plantation Nature Preserve

Mountain Island Lake

Mt. Holly-Huntersville Rd.

South Fork Catawba River

Rocky River

LAKE NORMAN STATE PARK

Lake Norman State Park, formerly Duke Power State Park, encompasses more than 1,400 acres of forested rolling lands along the eastern shore of Lake Norman's north end in Iredell County, North Carolina.

The park's hiking trails include 6.7-mile Lakeshore Trail that follows the shoreline of Lake Norman and offers excellent views of the reservoir; the 0.8-mile Alder Trail connecting the parking area to a peninsula with views of the backwater areas of the reservoir. Both trails feature wildflowers in spring, colors in fall, lakeside recreation, and important piedmont wildlife habitats. The park staff provide year-around natural history programs, including the Environmental Educational Learning Experience designed to educate youth about aquatic ecology and water-quality protection.

In addition to Lake Norman, the park has a smaller lake that offers good fishing for largemouth bass and sunfish. Boating on the lake is limited to canoes and rowboats, and there are boats usually available for rent during the summer months. Boat ramps provide access to Lake Norman and its good fishing for striped bass, largemouth bass, catfish, and crappie. Bank fishing on both lakes is permitted.

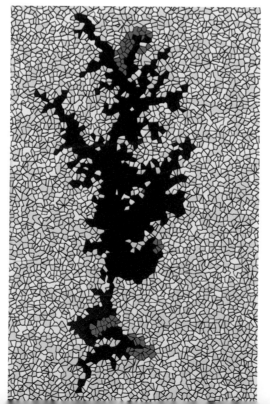

The park has two picnic areas. One area includes a shelter that can accommodate 125 people and has twenty picnic tables scattered through the forest. The second picnic area has thirty tables in addition to grills and drinking water. Camping facilities include thirty-three tent campsites without recreational vehicle hookups and two group campsites reserved for youth organizations. The campgrounds are closed during the winter.

The North Carolina Division of Parks and Recreation manages the park; call (704) 528-6350 for additional information. Access to the park, just ten miles south of Statesville, is off of I-77 at Exit 42, through Troutman.

JETTON PARK

Jetton Park is a 106-acre day-use area on the eastern shore of Lake Norman in northern Mecklenburg County, North Carolina. It is the perfect location for a stroll or picnic. Jetton Park is a formal, woodland park, an ideal place for an outing of groups of all sizes.

There are stands of mature loblolly pine and hardwood trees on the grounds, with an understory of native shrubs as habitat for many songbirds. Trails provide excellent bird-watching opportunities. Many of the park's facilities for tennis, hiking, bicycling, and

picnicking are nestled in scenic settings with Lake Norman as a backdrop. The park's trails offer pleasant bicycling and walking opportunities; bikes may be rented on the weekends and a children's playground is also available. Picnic sites and decks overlooking the lake provide ideal places for group get-togethers. Picnic decks for larger groups and a large, covered space called Waterfront Hall are available on a rental basis.

The Mecklenburg County Parks and Recreation Department manages the park; call (704) 896-9808 for additional information. Access to the park is from Jetton Road, off of NC 73.

Above, Mushrooms on log, and Gentian
Left, Inviting entrance into Jetton Park
Opposite, Dual tents for parents and children
at Lake Norman State Park.

LATTA PLANTATION NATURE PRESERVE

Almost within the shadow of Charlotte's skyline, Latta Plantation Nature Preserve includes 1,290 acres of upland and bottomland forests, fields, streams, and lakeshore habitats. The preserve shares space with three other facilities: The Latta Plantation Equestrian Center provides horseback riding opportunities and hosts special events; the Carolina Raptor Center houses a large number of injured eagles, owls, and hawks and educates the public about birds of prey while rehabilitating injured raptors for eventual return to the wild; and the historic Latta Plantation, the former home of James and Jane Knox Latta, serves as a living history house and farm. This site was the center of a cotton plantation in the early 1800s, and it is one of the best-preserved examples of the era of early settlement in the piedmont.

There are more than eighteen miles of hiking and bridle trails. A diversity of opportunities are offered by the preserve's trails: Some trails lead to old growth forests dominated by large American beech and oaks, and others go to Gar Creek and its bottomland forest, or to the Buzzards Rock overlook beside Mountain Island Lake, and to other lakeside areas. A well-marked educational trail offers information about the history of the forest. Wildflowers and ferns are seasonally common along sections of these walkways.

One of the preserve's major functions is to protect the plants and wildlife of the area. The National Audubon Society included the preserve as a notable

Above, Festivities at the Latta Plantation
Left, The historic Latta House, an antebellum home with reactivated well at Latta Plantation
Opposite, The Carolina Raptor Center for injured birds of prey

segment of the Mountain Island Lake Important Bird Area. A piedmont prairie is being restored to help protect the endangered Schweinitz's sunflower, a tall showy and very rare component of our native flora. Overall, a rich diversity of birds, mammals, reptiles and amphibians live in the area. Educational programs, scheduled through the preserve's Nature Center, provide opportunities to learn about these animals and their behavior and habitats.

Mecklenburg County Parks and Recreation Department manages the preserve; phone (704) 875-1391 for more information. To reach the Latta Plantation and Preserve, take Beatties Ford Road (SR 2074) less than one mile north of the intersection of Mount Holly-Huntersville Road (NC 27) with Beatties Ford Road; Sample Road (SR 2125) goes directly into Latta Plantation from Beatties Ford Road.

Mountain Island Lake Educational State Forest

This 1,200-acre tract along six miles of shoreline of Mountain Island Lake contains upland and bottomland forest communities as well as extensive wetland areas. Owned by Lincoln and Gaston Counties, the area will be managed by the North Carolina Division of Forest Resources, and plans for public access and educational programs are now being formulated. The tract is just north and east of the NC 16 bridge over Mountain Island Lake. The area is currently undeveloped, and the best way to access it is from the water along the upper end of Mountain Island Lake.

This forest is part of the Mountain Island Important Bird Area as identified by The National Audubon Society. A tour along the lakeside during the right seasons rewards visitors with views of green herons, great blue herons, and egrets feeding in the shallows; kingfishers and osprey diving for fish in the open waters; and numerous songbirds making use of the dense cover vegetation. Muskrats, beavers, and river otters are also shoreline residents. Wetlands are alive with chorus frogs and spring peepers in late winter and early spring. These areas also serve as egg-laying habitat for the beautiful marbled and spotted salamanders.

Left, A trail in an old growth forest in Latta Plantation
Opposite, The shore of Mountain Island Lake

While no facilities are in place at this time, the North Carolina Division of Forest Resources plans to build a visitor center, interpretive trails, and demonstration areas. The property will be available for research on forest resources, and demonstration areas will include forestry practices and soil, water, and wildlife conservation projects. Multiple-use forestry concepts will be researched at the site. The proposed facilities and lands will be available for youth and teacher education. Particularly because of its proximity to the urban areas of Charlotte and Gastonia, this tract, in time, will offer the opportunity for thousands of local citizens to learn about the region's valuable and magnificent forest resources.

The North Carolina Division of Forest Resources manages the property; for information call (704) 827-7576. To reach the forest, exit I-85 to NC 16. The property extends from just north and east of the NC 16 bridge over Mountain Island Lake. At present, the best way to see the property is by boat from Mountain Island Lake.

Cowans Ford Wildlife Refuge

Cowans Ford Wildlife Refuge encompasses more than 650 acres of forest, fields, and wetlands along the eastern shore of Mountain Island Lake in Mecklenburg County, North Carolina. The refuge, about ten miles north of Charlotte, is managed by the county's Parks and Recreation Department for the specific purpose of protecting and enhancing wildlife and wildlife habitats of the piedmont region.

The abundance of wildlife associated with Mountain Island Lake can be found in the refuge. Almost 200 species of birds have been documented in this area, and a large number of waterfowl overwinter here. White-tailed deer, wild turkeys, and other game species are often seen in the refuge's fields and woodlands. Numerous species of amphibians breed in the refuge's wetland habitats. The refuge has been designated a Wildlife Viewing Area as part of the national Watchable Wildlife Initiative.

Opposite, The forest of Mountain Island slowly rejuvenates
Above, left, Gentian; Middle, A rat snake awaits prey; Right, Bloodroot

There are wildlife viewing stands accessible to the public. These provide views of open fields, ponds, and forest edge habitats. While public access to most of the refuge is restricted in order to avoid disturbing wildlife, refuge personnel provide access to these areas through scheduled guided tours.

Mecklenburg County Parks and Recreation manages Cowans Ford Refuge; call (704) 875-1391 for more information. To reach the refuge, take I-77 (north from Charlotte), exit to NC 73, then drive west to Beatties Ford Road (SR 2128), south to Neck Road (SR 2074), and west to the refuge.

Above, Buckeye; Above left, Wildlife viewing platform at Cowans Ford Refuge
Above right, Study groups research and discourse
Opposite, An expansive wetland for animals and waterfowl alike

CHAPTER SIX

LOWER CATAWBA RIVER

Opposite, Public fishing and walking pier at McDowell Nature Preserve on Lake Wylie

McDowell Nature Preserve

Charlotte

Shopton Rd.

485

160

55

Lake
Wylie

York

Monroe

181

Sugar Creek

5

Catawba River

52 1

75

Rock Hill

200

Fishing Creek

5

321

77

21

Old Hickory Road

72

Landsford Canal State Park

9

Catawba River

9

Lancaster

9

Chester

72

9

Rocky Creek

52 1

Little Rocky Creek

Fishing Creek
Reservoir

321

52 1

21

77

Wateree
Lake

Lake Wateree State Park

ree Estate Road

4   0   4   8 Miles

N
W   E
S

McDowell Nature Preserve

This 1,000-acre nature preserve protects expanses of mature hardwood forests along the Mecklenburg County, North Carolina, shore of Lake Wylie, southwest of Charlotte. While most visitors to McDowell Nature Preserve may sense that the preserve primarily consists of readily accessible areas near the roadway, more than 90 percent of McDowell is undeveloped.

The preserve protects and showcases some of the finest upland hardwood forest stands in the central piedmont region. Small streams run over bedrock and gravel substrates, and there are exceptional displays of spring wildflowers and trees of great size. The forests are also habitat for a great diversity of mammal, amphibian, reptile, and bird species.

Nine nature trails, totaling more than 6.5 miles, take hikers to a variety of settings. Some trails lead to shady cove-forested areas of mature hardwood stands of red and white oaks, American beech, shagbark hickory, tulip poplar, and red maple. These cove forests also harbor springtime wildflowers and ferns, including wild geraniums, jack-in-the-pulpit, foamflower, sweet shrub, maidenhair fern, wild azalea, and blue star. Other trails

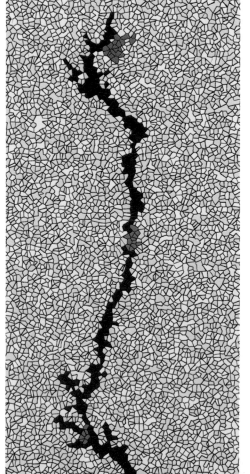

lead to drier ridgetops with stands of pine and red cedar. Several trails follow scenic woodland streams, while others lead to lakeside vistas.

The best starting place for visitors is the McDowell Nature Center. The center offers nature displays and information about the park and its trails. It also has a well-equipped classroom and a gift counter. McDowell offers overnight camping and excellent opportunities for picnicking, fishing, and other activities.

The Mecklenburg County Parks and Recreation Department manages the area. Call the park office at (704) 588-5224 for more information. Access to the park is off NC 49, just east of Buster Boyd Bridge.

Landsford Canal State Park

Landsford Canal State Park is on a beautiful section of the Catawba River where the river drops thirty-five feet in elevation over a two mile-long stretch of rapids. This 450-acre riverside park is 15 miles south of Rock Hill, in Chester and Lancaster Counties, South Carolina.

The shallow shoals here have lured people and wildlife to the area for centuries. Today, through the

protective management and the interpretive programs and displays provided by the South Carolina Department of Parks, Recreation and Tourism, the public can learn about important historical events that have occurred in this area, while observing wildlife species.

Land's Ford has been a landmark in this region since Native Americans first used the shallow rapids as a ford. The ford was also used by Scotch-Irish settlers migrating into the Carolinas during the mid-1700s. During the Revolutionary War, Lord Cornwallis crossed the river with his troops on the march from

Above, The Rocky Shoals Spider Lily—a rare plant which makes Landsford Canal famous
Left, Handicapped accessible platform to a forest stream at McDowell Nature Preserve (Lake Wylie)
Opposite, Wading in the shoals of the Catawba River at Landsford Canal State Park

The Lower Catawba River

Above, Flowering Devil's Bit among ferns, McDowell Nature Preserve

Opposite, Casual family fishing in Lake Wateree State Park

Above, Picnicking on the banks of the Catawba River at Landsford Canal State Park

Charlotte to Winnsboro after the loss to Americans at the 1780 battle of Kings Mountain. General William R. Davie, who fought with General Thomas Sumter, the "Gamecock" and for whom Sumter National Forest is named, had a home on the side of the ford. The ford was used again during the Civil War when some of Sherman's troops crossed the river in their march through South Carolina in 1865.

Above, Butterfly Weed
Right, An eagle and chick make their home in the park

Construction of a 1.5-mile long canal around the shallow rapids in the Land's Ford area began in 1819. The Landsford Canal was to be part of a system of canals that would enable easier passage of cotton boats to Charleston. A number of notable people were involved in the planning and construction of the canal. It was built under the general direction of Joel Poinsett, a diplomat and president of the Board of Public Works (and an amateur naturalist, for whom the Poinsettia is named). Washington Monument architect Robert Mills was the engineer for the canal, and the builder was Robert Leckie, who later did the stonework for the Botanical Gardens in Washington, D.C.

The canal at Land's Ford was completed in 1823, but it did not receive great use because the development of railroads became the dominant form of transportation of market goods. By 1840 the canal was no longer in use. Today the canal at Land's Ford is one of the best preserved of these historic structures in South Carolina.

In addition to the historic canals, Landsford Canal State Park protects a treasure trove of natural resources. Visitors can observe bald eagles that nest in the park, as well as many species of hawks and wading birds. The largest known colony of the Rocky Shoals Spider Lily, a rare beautiful plant, occurs within the rapids at the park. This showy species blooms during late May or early June and provides one of the most spectacular natural sights in the southeastern United States.

There are great views of the Catawba River, an interpretive hiking trail along the river, and a picnic area; a shelter can be reserved. There is also fishing and canoeing on the river and informative displays about the historic canal.

The South Carolina Department of Parks, Recreation and Tourism manages the area; call the park office at (803) 789-5800 for additional information. To reach the park from I-77, take Exit 65; drive east on SC 9, turn left (northeast) onto SC 223 to US 21; turn left onto County Road S-330.

Lake Wateree State Park

This 238-acre state park, on the western shore of Lake Wateree, is off of US 21, in Fairfield County, South Carolina. Many visitors use the park to access Lake Wateree, a recreational reservoir that provides an excellent year-round fishery.

Above, Squaw Root
Opposite, Public pier onto Lake Wateree

The parklands, like much of the surrounding countryside in this area of South Carolina, were routinely planted in cotton in the early part of the 20th century. Now reforested, these park forests support various species of wildlife including white-tailed deer, gray fox, wild turkey, songbirds, reptiles, and amphibians. Red-shouldered and red-tailed hawks are commonly seen and heard here. Wetlands associated with Lake Wateree are adjacent to the park and contain extensive shallows dominated by cattails, buttonbush, and other aquatic plants. Some of the best wildlife watching opportunities are associated with these shallow areas. Great blue herons, egrets, and other fish-eating birds are readily observed here. In the early spring months, frogs, including spring peepers and leopard frogs, can be heard "singing" from these shallow areas.

The park has campsites, a nature trail, a picnic area, and a playground. An excellent launching facility provides boat access to Lake Wateree.

The South Carolina Department of Parks, Recreation and Tourism manages the area, and the park's office number is (803) 482-6401. To reach the park, take I-77, Exit 41. Go east on secondary road SSR 41 to US 21; turn left on US 21 to secondary road SSR 101; turn right onto SSR 101, and drive approximately 5 miles to the park.

Right, Cardinal flower

Opposite, Reflections of trees and egrets on Lake Wateree

Above, Pinesap thrives on the rich forest floor

Right, New life in the forest

Opposite, Golden fall in the mist

DISCARD